THE

POISONOUS SNAKES OF INDIA

THE POISONOUS SNAKES OF INDIA.

FOR

THE USE OF THE OFFICIALS AND OTHERS

RESIDING IN

THE INDIAN EMPIRE.

BY

JOSEPH EWART

GYAN

Published by

Gyan Publishing House
5, Ansari Road
Daryaganj, New Delhi-110002
Phone: 011-47034999, 9811692060
E-mail: books@gyanbooks.com

Distribution Network
gyanbooks.com
India, USA, Canada, UK, Australia, France

ISBN: 978-93-6433-104-3 (PB)

First Published, 1878

2nd Impression 2023

Printed at: Gyan Press, Delhi.

THE POISONOUS SNAKES OF INDIA

Author: JOSEPH EWART

THE

POISONOUS SNAKES OF INDIA.

FOR

THE USE OF THE OFFICIALS AND OTHERS

RESIDING IN

THE INDIAN EMPIRE.

COMPILED BY

JOSEPH EWART, M.D., M.R.C.P., LOND.

SURGEON MAJOR IN THE BENGAL ARMY;
PROFESSOR OF PHYSIOLOGY IN THE MEDICAL COLLEGE;
SURGEON TO THE GENERAL HOSPITAL, AND FELLOW OF THE UNIVERSITY OF CALCUTTA;
PRESIDENT OF THE SNAKE POISON COMMISSION;
FELLOW OF THE ZOOLOGICAL SOCIETY, LONDON;
PRESIDENT OF THE BENGAL SOCIAL SCIENCE ASSOCIATION;
LATE ACTING PRINCIPAL AND PROFESSOR OF MEDICINE, AND SENIOR PHYSICIAN, CALCUTTA MEDICAL COLLEGE AND HOSPITAL.

LONDON:
J. & A. CHURCHILL, NEW BURLINGTON STREET.
1878.

PREFACE.

THE object contemplated in publishing this small work (which may be viewed as a supplement to Sir Joseph Fayrer's magnificent "Thanatophidia of India") has been to place in the hands of the busy officials of India a handy-book, by means of which they may easily recognise any of the poisonous reptiles of the Peninsula. Sir Joseph Fayrer, K.C.S.I., when applied to, generously sanctioned the use of the beautiful plates figured in his Thanatophidia.

The scientific descriptions of Günther, Fayrer, and Anderson have been preserved; but as all technical and other difficult terms have been fully explained in the Glossary, the text may be regarded as capable of being made intelligible to the mind of the ordinary reader. Any further attempt at popularising the work would have ended in redundancy, and rendered brevity and portability impossible. There is scarcely a term employed in the descriptions, which cannot at once be understood by a reference to the Glossary. The conciseness thus accomplished has enabled me generally to place the descriptions side by side with the Plates. This is a great advantage to men so fully employed as are the civil, medical, and police authorities of India.

It is believed that this work will meet a real want. It will enable the hard-worked civil surgeon to identify, without much trouble, poisonous snakes, a matter of great import to him in the practice of his profession, and in his capacity as—it may be—the sole medical jurisprude in his district. It will also enable the English speaking and reading officials of all grades and departments to distinguish poisonous from non-poisonous snakes. It is further hoped that it will obviate the necessity of paying rewards for the capture and destruction of innocent snakes, as has frequently been done, and thus prevent the unnecessary expenditure of the public funds.

The few brief suggestions concerning treatment, down to the end of the 7th paragraph, if adopted by the non-professional persons brought into contact with those who have been poisoned, might lead to the saving of much human life. Thus there is some reason for supposing that, if the ligatures and other means recommended were applied instantly after a person has been bitten, that the absorption of the poison would be prevented or materially lessened; and that the surgeon would be placed under favourable circumstances for combating the dreadful enemy he has been summoned to oppose. Another point is that, in all probability, the excisions that were formerly practised have neither been extensive nor deep enough. My confrère, Dr. Wall, has, I believe, undertaken some most interesting experiments on the point, with a view to determine the area over which the poison is diffused from an ordinary bite, in different regions of the body. I believe the result will go to prove the absolute necessity for far more extensive excisions than have hitherto been considered needful. The minor amputations of a toe or a finger, and the large and deep excisions recommended in other parts of the body, when promptly undertaken and executed are incomparably lesser evils than those which must be encountered if any dregs of the snake poison are left behind to infect the blood, and eventually to cause almost certain death.

CONTENTS AND LIST OF PLATES.

SUBSCRIPTION LIST.

Government of India	115	Copies.
,, Madras	50	,,
,, Bombay	50	,,
,, Bengal	200	,,
,, North-West Provinces	120	,,
,, Punjab	100	,,
,, Oude	50	,,
,, British Burmah	50	,,
,, Assam	30	,,
,, Ceylon	20	,,
,, Cape of Good Hope	100	,,
Agent Governor-General, Rajputana	6	,,
,, ,, Hydrabad	20	,,
,, ,, Kashmir	10	,,
Chief Commissioner of Scinde	20	,,
Resident at Court of Travancore and Cochin	12	,,
,, Baroda	23	,,
,, Gwalior	2	,,
,, Jeypore	20	,,
,, Kishenghur	2	,,
Total	1000	Copies.

THE

POISONOUS SNAKES OF INDIA.

SYMPTOMS AND TREATMENT OF SNAKE POISONING.

Local.—When a person is effectively bitten by a poisonous snake, he feels a stinging sensation in the part penetrated. This is soon followed by pain, at first of a dull, aching, and subsequently, of a lancinating and piercing, character. The ultimate and rather rapid effect is numbness terminating in local paralysis of sensation. There may also be slight swelling. In poisoning by the cobra, daboia, and other terrestrial snakes, there will usually be found the marks or points, sometimes indicated by a small film of clotted blood, where the two fangs have entered half an inch or more apart. Or, as in the case of a finger being bitten, there may only be one point of penetration, the other fang having missed altogether. At a later period the part assumes a leaden or livid hue, due in great part to the effusion of blood beneath the skin (ecchymosis). When the bite has been inflicted by a salt-water snake, the fang-marks are more difficult to distinguish; because the fangs are not much larger than the fish-like teeth situated immediately behind them. There may, further, be marks or scratches of some of the teeth as well as of the fangs. As the poison gains access to the blood, the general symptoms affecting the whole nervous organisation soon divert attention from, and eclipse, the local indications. Unless the ligature has been applied at once or very soon after an effective bite these very soon make their appearance.

General.—Very soon after an effective bite, where the ligature has been delayed or not applied at all, the poison is absorbed into the blood, and makes its presence felt upon the great nerve-centres of the cord and medulla. The patient is extremely restless and excited. His alarm amounts to horror, intensified by a deeply-rooted conviction of the utter hopelessness of his case. As the first signs of nervous depression, languor and muscular exhaustion make their appearance, the emotional excitement becomes increased, and, at an early period, the feeling is one of despair. The face is pallid, and covered with drops of perspiration; pupils dilated; pulse quickened; there is loss of appetite, nausea or vomiting. General muscular paralysis eventually supervenes; there is lethargy and drowsiness, ending in unconsciousness, accompanied or followed by involuntary evacuations, which are sometimes tinged with blood. The breathing becomes slow, laboured and shallow; pupils widely dilated. The body becomes bathed in cold, clammy perspiration; the pulse remains full, quick and compressible. The respiration is gradually stopped, and death is ushered in by convulsions, or convulsive twitchings of the muscles of the extremities and face. The pulse beats a few minutes (from three to four) after all breathing has ceased.

In some cases, where a person has been bitten by an exhausted snake, or by one whose aggregate supply of poison is small, as is the case in the tiger snake of Australia, or by a vigorous cobra, from which, owing to some cause or other, only a minute quantity of poison has been injected; or where a person has been greatly protected against the absorption of the poison by the early application of the ligature, the above symptoms may be present only in a modified degree. Recovery from the general symptoms may take place. The consequences in the part infected may cause much trouble; but these are to be dealt with by the surgeon on general principles.

Treatment.

1. A. *By non-professional persons.*—Whenever a person has been bitten by a poisonous reptile, issue orders at once for the attendance of a medical practitioner.

2. Pending his arrival, if the bite has been inflicted in the upper or lower extremities, promptly arrest absorption of the poison by immediately applying a strong cord very tightly round the limb, about a couple of inches above the bitten part, and two or more cords, from four or six inches apart, twisted as tightly as possible, higher up the limb. Thus, if a finger be bitten at the tip, the first ligature may be applied to the base of the digit, the second to the wrist, and the third to the middle of the forearm; in like manner, if the end of a toe be bitten, the first cord should be secured round the base of the toe; the second round the instep, and the

third a few inches above the ankle. In bites higher up the extremities, the ligatures should be employed, at suitable distances from each other, with the utmost promptitude. Sir Joseph Fayrer recommends the insertion of a piece of stick or other lever between the cord and the limb or member, with a view to twist the ligature to the utmost.

3. Carefully identify the punctures made by the fangs of the snake. Excise the part with a sharp penknife to the extent of a finger-nail, if the bite is on a finger or toe, if possible, round each puncture, and deeply, almost down to the bone, or in depth from a quarter to half an inch. Scarify freely the circumference of the wound, and encourage bleeding. Wash and squeeze it effectively to expel poison. Then apply to the bottom of the wound a red-hot iron so as to cauterise and kill the adjacent soft tissues so that they may be incapable of absorbing any poison that may not have been removed by the excision or destroyed by the cautery.

4. As the soft parts at the ends of the fingers and toes are comparatively dense, and the diffusion of the poison consequently limited, the extent of the excisions should be proportionately restricted. But if the fangs have penetrated the skin of any part of the extremities above, such as the leg, thigh, forearm, or upper arm, the extent of the diffusion of the poison is much greater, owing to the looser texture of the areolar tissue in these regions. The excision of the poisoned tissues must therefore be considerably extended and deeper. The scarification of the margins at the bottom of the wound and the cauterisation, either with a red-hot iron or live coal, must also be applied with more freedom. If the bite has been inflicted by the daboia, it may be needful even to excise muscular tissue, as well as skin and areolar tissue; because the fangs of this viper are much longer and penetrate deeper than those of the cobra.

5. It will often happen that absorption of poison to a greater or less extent may have occurred before the ligatures have been applied. In such cases they must not be relaxed; because their relaxation will admit the ingress of more poison into the blood. By keeping them firmly adjusted, we may hope, if they have been applied early enough, that such a limitation of the absorption of the poison may have been effected as to conduce materially to the preservation of life; whilst by their premature removal, the renewal of the absorption may, even in cases where only a small quantity of the virus has been thus introduced, turn the balance irretrievably against the patient and cause a rapidly fatal issue.

6. Doubtless mortification of the parts below the ligatures may be caused, if they are retained beyond from half an hour to an hour; but, in patients who have been effectively bitten by any of the venomous snakes described in this work, the danger to life from mortification, which can easily be dealt with by the surgeon in due course, is not to be compared to that to be encountered by the uncontrolled absorption of the poison into the blood. In the first case, life may be saved; in the second, judging from the vast experience of Sir Joseph Fayrer and others, death is almost certain to follow.

7. In addition to the above measures, which, notwithstanding their apparent severity, are nevertheless merciful and humane, moderate doses of stimulants may be given until the physician or surgeon arrives. Thus fifteen drops of pure liquor ammoniæ in an ounce of water may be administered every twenty minutes, until three or four doses are taken. For a similar purpose a table-spoonful of brandy, rum, whisky, or arrack thoroughly distilled in a wineglassful of water may be given from time to time until, say, a couple of ounces have been swallowed. It is doubtful whether any good is derived from over-stimulation; under- is better than over-stimulation. Thus care must be taken not to push the doses of alcohol in the shape of brandy, rum, whisky, or arrack, so as to produce inebriation. During the exhibition of stimulants, nourishment in a liquid form—animal soups, and milk, or eggs beaten up with brandy, &c., should be employed. If the depression and feeling of sinking be marked, mustard plasters should be applied to the region of the heart or pit of the stomach, or over the medulla, behind the nape of the neck, or to all three regions at once. No apparent benefit is derived from compelling the patient to move about; on the contrary, such enforced exertion increases the tendency to exhaustion. Give the patient rest in a cool and thoroughly well-ventilated room, protected from the sun; he should be fanned with the punkah if needful. All these measures may be had recourse to by even untrained persons. Some of the means suggested are certainly most severe, "and not such as under any other circumstances should be entrusted to non-professional persons; but the alternative is so dreadful that, even at the risk of unskilful treatment, it is better that the patient should have this chance of recovery."—(Fayrer.) Galvanism to the heart and diaphragm, and the Sylvester and Marshall Hall methods of artificial respiration have also been recommended in cases where the prostration is extreme.

8. B. *By the Surgeon.*—In many cases the surgeon, on arrival, often finds himself placed under circumstances of the greatest responsibility and difficulty. Presuming that the foregoing measures have been adopted with efficiency and promptitude after the bite, and that symptoms of poisoning are consequently in abeyance, he should carefully examine the ligatures and see that they are tightened sufficiently to prevent absorption, and also the wound made by the excision, in order to ascertain whether it is wide and deep enough to facilitate the extraction of the whole of the poison or the total destruction of the remainder by the live coal or the actual cautery. In a case of this kind he will have time to find out whether the snake which inflicted the injury was, in all human probability, a poisonous one or not. If he be satisfied that the bite was inflicted by a poisonous reptile—especially by a cobra or daboia—and that it was an effective one, he is called upon, in a preponderating majority of instances, without the chance of a consultation with another surgeon, to decide on the spur of the moment as to the course to be pursued. He may reason somewhat in this way: "If the ligatures be removed, absorption will set in; the blood will be charged with a fatal quantity of the poison; the functions of the great nerve-centres will be destroyed; the respiration will cease, and soon after the circulation also, cotemporaneously with actual death. It is true that mortification will be prevented, but then this comparatively insignificant gain at the best will only be temporary, and attained at the sacrifice of the life of the patient. On the other hand, it is quite clear that little or no poison has as yet gained access to the blood and the great nerve-centres, and that, to maintain this desirable condition, one of two things must be done; either the ligatures must be kept on until all chance of absorption be removed by gangrene, and the patient thus exposed to other risks of blood-poisoning, such as pyæmia, and a protracted convalescence ending sooner or later in amputation; or the poisoned member must be removed two or three inches or more above the site of the bite." In the case of fingers and toes, where the bite has been proved to be effective either by the existence of the fang-marks or unimpeachable testimony, there ought to be no hesitation as to the procedure to be adopted—viz., immediate amputation. These minor amputations are generally unattended with much danger to life; whilst, if an attempt be made to save the member, life is almost certain to be lost. By amputation

before the symptoms of poisoning have become developed, owing to the prevention of absorption by the successful application of the ligatures, life may often be saved. And I am persuaded it will be usually so saved if the ligatures, excisions, and cautery have all been employed immediately after the poisoning has taken place, and also in many cases where only a very small quantity of poison has been poured into the soft parts or into the blood.

9. In poisoning of fingers and toes, where, either from delay in the application of the ligatures, &c., or from their not having been used at all, the symptoms of snake poisoning have become unmistakably pronounced, when the surgeon arrives upon the scene, the question whether amputation is justifiable naturally arises, not because there is much risk attending the procedure itself, but because, as may be argued, all operative measures may be regarded as utterly hopeless. Under such circumstances the surgeon is again placed in a situation where self-reliance and prompt decision are all-important. In cases of this kind there has probably been too much delay and hesitation already, caused by ignorance as to the measures to be adopted, or dismay at the injury which has been inflicted. Neither the one nor the other can be permitted to influence the surgeon. He may, however, reason in this way: "Life is in imminent danger, and death will probably follow, do what he may. Perhaps sufficient poison has been introduced into the circulation to produce all the signs of snake poisoning, but not enough to prove fatal, provided the ingress of fresh supplies be promptly prohibited. Thus, although a successful result is problematical, amputation is clearly the only hopeful proceeding." The part bitten should be at once isolated by the ligature if this has not been done already, and the member removed, in order to cut off all fresh supplies of the poison. When I was serving with the Meywar Bheel Corps, at Kherwarrah, near Oodeypore, a Hindoo was brought to me, having been bitten on the end of the thumb by a full-grown cobra. After getting up in the morning, he had put his hand into a gurrah, or earthen vessel, to remove something it contained. A cobra, which was secreted in the vessel, seized him by the thumb. The snake was secured and brought with the patient. He was presented to me half an hour after the accident. The marks of the fangs were identified. The native doctor had seen him a few minutes after the bite, and had applied a stout cord round the thumb at two places.

But the man was faint, depressed, nauseated, and prostrated. After seeing that the ligatures were tightened as firmly as possible, I asked the Brahmin native doctor to prevail upon the patient to let me take off his thumb, and so save his life. The thumb was first chopped off to economise time through the first phalanx, and subsequently amputated in the usual way at the metacarpo-phalangeal joint. He passed through a stage of severe nervous prostration, with intense nausea, vomiting and diarrhœa with bloody evacuations; but eventually rallied, and made a good recovery.

10. When the bite has been made on the forearm or leg, the upper arm or thigh, the ligatures, excision and the cautery may be practised more frequently, without having recourse to amputation. Because, in most cases, unless indeed the poison, as occasionally happens, is poured directly and *en masse* into a vein or artery, a sufficient quantity of the soft parts can easily be removed, so as to include the whole area of the poisoned district. The extent of the excised area must depend upon the depth of the skin and subcutaneous areolar tissue, the density of the infected areolar tissue, and the length of the penetrating fangs of the snake. Over the shin the depth of skin and areolar tissue is small; over the thigh the depth is greater, the cellular tissue is loose, and more easily penetrated by fluid, such as snake poison. Thus, in the former situation, both the area and depth of the excised part would be less than in the latter regions, because the area of its diffusion would be less. Over the shin, the depth of the excision should be down to the periosteum, and to the muscles on either side, and it should embrace an area of a square inch or more. In the thigh, the excision should be down at least to the fascia covering the muscles, and ought to be even more extensive, including an area of a couple of square inches or so. There is reason to believe that one reason why excision has not been attended with the expected success, has arisen from the fact that all the infected tissue has not been removed. It is manifest that, if any be left behind, the remaining poison may be insidiously absorbed, and eventually destroy life. Then again, if the bite has been inflicted by the daboia, on a thin and spare individual, the muscles of the calf or thigh may be penetrated. And, in such a case, muscle, in addition to skin and areolar tissue, may have to be excised.

11. Amputation here is in itself a grave proceeding, and it is fortunate that it is not primarily involved in the consideration of the case. Provided the ligatures have been tightened to the utmost, time will be allowed in which to make the excision so extensive and deep as to embrace the whole of the infected area; to resemble, in truth, in principle at least, and in completeness, the small and comparatively unimportant amputation of the fingers or toes. But it will often happen that gangrene will have resulted from the ligature, and, as a secondary measure, amputation will become needful. A case of this kind occurred to me at the Calcutta General Hospital. The patient, a Mohammedan, had been bitten in the forearm by a daboia. Ligatures and the cautery were applied. Gangrene supervened. He was admitted under my care. The soft parts, up to within half an inch of the axilla, were destroyed by sloughing and gangrene. Enough skin over the deltoid remained for a flap. The arm was taken off at the shoulder-joint, and the patient made an excellent recovery.

12. When an effective bite has been inflicted on any part of the trunk, the ligature cannot be employed. But excision and the cautery, if done at once, may be the means of saving life. In these cases sufficient time usually elapses to permit the absorption of a fatal quantity of poison before the arrival of the surgeon. It may sometimes happen, where only a limited quantity of poison has been injected, that, even after the signs of snake poisoning have been fairly developed, the complete extirpation of the infected parts may succeed in saving life, which would otherwise be sacrificed.

13. It is much to be regretted that the intravenous injection of ammonia first introduced by Fontana and the Italians, and energetically revived by Professor Halford, of Melbourne, has not been found (by the Calcutta Snake Poison Commission) to be of any practical use in dogs poisoned by Indian or Australian snakes. Nor does the liquor potassæ recommended to be injected into the blood by Dr. Short, of Madras, apparently do much good. It might do more if injected freely into the poisoned part.

Sir Joseph Fayrer recommends that liquor ammoniæ, nitric acid, carbolic acid, strong whipcord, and a small sharp knife be kept at all police stations for immediate use in cases of snake poisoning.

NAJA TRIPUDIANS.

Plate I

Kovah Gokurrah

Length including tail,	5′ 0″.
Length of tail,	9″.
Girth,	5½″.

Hanhart Chromolith

Drawn by Annoda Prosad Bagchee, Student. *Govt Sch. of Art, Calcutta*

N A J A.

Naja Tripudians—Cobra—Cobra di Capello.

Naja.—The following description is given of the genus by Günther:—"Body and tail of moderate length; belly flat; head rather high and short, not very distinct from neck, which is very dilatable, the anterior ribs being elongate. The shields of the head normal, but the loreal is absent. Nostrils wide, lateral, between two shields; eye of moderate size, with round pupil. One præ-, three, sometimes two or four post-oculars. Six upper labials, the third and fourth entering the orbit; the third forms the lower half of the anterior margin of the orbit. Scales smooth, much imbricate, in numerous series round the hood. Anal entire. Sub-caudals two-rowed. The fang is grooved, with foramen at its extremity; one or two small ordinary teeth at a short distance behind it."

The manners and customs, &c., distribution and varieties of the genus are admirably described by Sir Joseph Fayrer in the following quotation from the Thanatophidia:—"There are several varieties, each having a distinct name given to it by the natives. They are all most deadly, and though the snake-charmers consider some more poisonous than others, it is probable that any difference that may exist is more due to the vigour of the individual snake than to anything attributable to the particular variety. They all have the hood, and never attack without distending it. They raise the anterior third of the body from the ground, slide slowly along on the posterior two-thirds, and with the hood dilated remain on the alert, darting the head forward to the attack when anything hostile approaches. This attitude is very striking, and few objects are more calculated to inspire awe than a large cobra, when with his hood erect, hissing loudly, and his eyes glaring, he prepares to strike. Nevertheless, they are not, I believe, aggressive; and unless interfered with or irritated, they crawl along the ground with the neck undilated, looking not unlike innocent snakes; but the moment they are disturbed, they assume the menacing attitude I have described.

"The *Naja Tripudians* (the only species), or Cobra, grows to the length of five feet and a half, or even more. On one occasion I received a living female cobra from Nagpore, C.P., sent by Dr. W. B. Beatson. It was of the variety called 'Kurrees Gokurrah,' of a light chocolate colour, without any mark on the hood. It was five feet eight inches long, including the tail, which measured eleven and a quarter inches. In girth it was six and a quarter inches. It was very powerful and fierce, and Dr. Beatson told me that it killed a fowl in one minute.

"This was the largest cobra I have seen, but I believe they attain even a greater size than this. The cobra is found all over Hindostan up to eight thousand feet high in the Himalaya; but Mr. Hodgson says he has never seen it in the Nepaul valley.* It is equally dreaded and fatal everywhere. The varieties are numerous, and they are distinguished by the markings on the hood, and by various shades of colour, from the darkest olive or black, with a purple iridescence, to a pale chocolate, fawn, or yellow colour. They are all, notwithstanding their differences of colour or marking, considered by naturalists to be but varieties of one species. They have various names in different parts of India, and are regarded by the snake-catchers as different species, and as having different powers of destruction. Such differences most likely depend on age, vigour, or other circumstances, as naturally the intensity of the poison of the different varieties is probably about equal.

"The cobra is a nocturnal snake—that is, it is most active in the night; but it is often seen moving about in the day. It is oviparous; the eggs, from eighteen to twenty-five in number, are obovate, and about the size of those of a pigeon; the shell is white, but tough and leathery. The cobras feed on small animals, birds' eggs, frogs, fish, or insects; they rob hen-roosts, and swallow the eggs whole; they prefer taking their food at dusk or in the night. They are said to drink a great deal of water; but it is certain that they will live weeks, even months, in captivity, without touching food or water. They go into

* Fayrer has seen it in the Oude Terai.

water readily, and swim well, but are essentially terrestrial snakes. They can climb, and occasionally ascend trees in search of food. Cobras are not unfrequently found in the roofs of huts, holes in walls, fowl houses, old ruins, under logs of wood, in cellars, old brick kilns, and old masonry of stone, brickwork, or mud. Such are the common dwelling-places of these reptiles, and where they are frequently disturbed by men, who, stepping on or inadvertently disturbing and touching them, receive their death-wound.

"The cobra is most deadly, and its poison, when thoroughly inoculated by a fresh and vigorous snake, is quickly fatal. Paralysis of the nerve-centres takes place, and death occurs with great rapidity, sometimes in a few minutes, especially when the fangs, having penetrated a vein, inoculate the poison immediately into the venous circulation. The number of deaths caused yearly in India by these snakes is perfectly appalling. The cases in which recovery occurs are, it is to be feared, very few; treatment appears to be of little avail unless it be almost immediate, and then, in the case of a genuine bite, there is but little hope of saving life. As to the mode of treatment and other matters connected with the bite of the cobra, and the great mortality caused by it in India, they will be described subsequently.

"The cobras are the favourites of the snake-charmers, and it is astonishing with what ease and freedom they are seized and handled by these men, even when in possession of their fangs. The snake-catchers render them temporarily harmless by cutting out the poison fangs; but these are quickly reproduced, unless, as most generally happens, with the fang all the reserve fangs and germs are removed, in which case the snake is harmless for life. Their graceful movements in the erect attitude they assume with the hood distended as they follow the movements of the snake-charmer's hands, make them an object of wonder as well as fear to all, and the superstitions of the natives about them are endless. The muntra, or spell, is far more potent in their idea than any drug, and to such they generally trust when bitten. How frequently these fail the records of any civil station in India will prove, and it is to be feared that the more material remedies of the physician are scarcely more potent for good.

"The snake-catchers in Bengal describe a great variety of cobras. The following list was furnished by a very intelligent Mohammedan, who has had much experience, and who, though not a snake-catcher originally by profession, has been one for several years, and is exceedingly expert in catching and handling these reptiles. The first great distinction made by these people is between cobras with spectacles on the hood, or 'Gokurrahs,' and those with one ocellus or other mark on the hood, named 'Keautiahs.' They maintain that these are distinct species, and that they vary considerably not only in appearance, but in habits and properties. Some gokurrahs, however, have no mark on the hood.

"The Gokurrah has the following varieties :—

"1. Kála, black ; 2. Koyah, black and white ; 3. Gomunah, wheat-coloured ; 4. Puddah, yellow coloured ; 5. Dudiah, whitish coloured ; 6. Tentuliah, tamarind seed coloured ; 7. Kurrees, earthy coloured ; 8. Tameshur, copper coloured ; 9. Puddun nág, golden coloured. The 2nd, 3rd, and 7th are the most common varieties about Calcutta.

"The Keautiah has the following :—

"1. Kála, black ; 2. Tentuliah, tamarind seed coloured ; 3. Kurrees, earthy coloured ; 4. Sonera, gold coloured ; 5. Dudiah, whitish coloured ; 6. Bans-buniah, mottled white and black ; 7. Giribungha, brownish coloured ; 8. Koyah, black and white coloured ; 9. Sankha-mookhi, like the Sankni or Bungarus fasciatus, black and yellow. The Cobra is called in many parts of Hindostan 'Kála samp,' 'Nág samp.' The 1st, 2nd, and 6th are most common about Calcutta, and no doubt in different parts of Bengal many other varieties are described, and different names are given to those above-mentioned, for the natives are fond of refining on points of this kind."

Plate 2

OPHIOPHAGUS ELAPS (HAMADRYAS) DUSKY VARIETY.

Length including tail	*11' 10"*
Length of tail	*13"*
Girth	*9"*

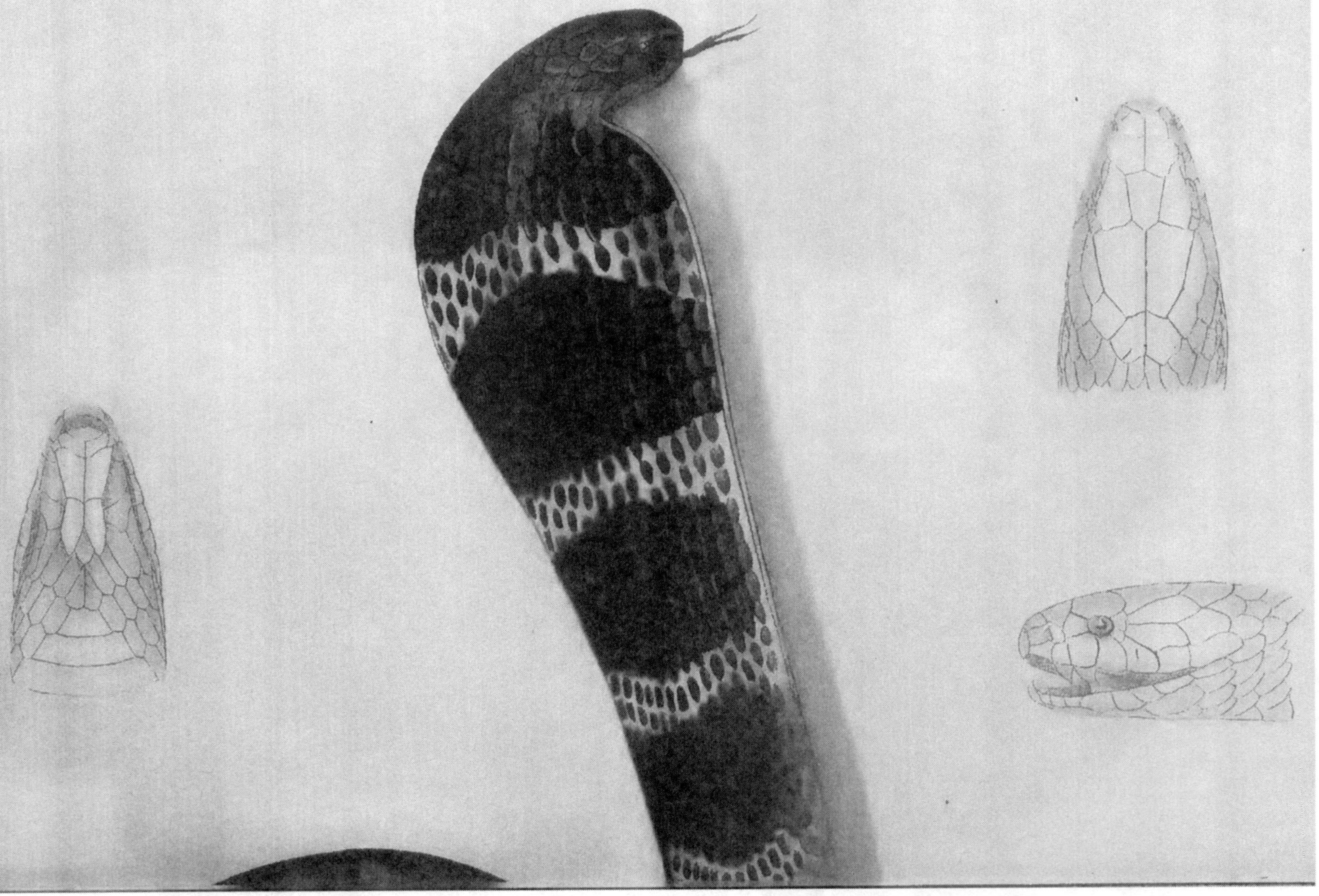

Drawn by Annoda Prosad Bagchee Student

Gov^{t} Sch. of Art. Calcutta

OPHIOPHAGUS.

Ophiophagus Elaps.

Hamadryad (Günther), Sunkerchor (Native), Ai ráj in Orissa (Fayrer). This is a hooded snake, varying in length, in the adult state, from twelve to fourteen feet. It is powerful, active, and aggressive.

Günther describes the genus as follows :—" Body rather elongate ; tail of proportionate length ; head rather short, depressed, scarcely distinct from neck, which is dilatable ; occipitals surrounded by three pairs of large shields, the two anterior of which are temporals. Nostril between two nasals. Loreal none ; one or two præ-, three post-oculars. Scales smooth, much imbricate, in transverse rows, in fifteen series round the body, but in many more round the neck ; those of the vertebral series are rather larger than the others, ventrals more than 200 ; anal entire ; anterior sub-caudals simple, posterior two-rowed, sometimes all bifid. Maxillary with a large fang in front, which is perforated at the end, showing a longitudinal groove in front ; a second small simple tooth at some distance behind the fang."

Varieties dependent upon " age and locality" :—

" α. Olive green above ; the shields of the head, the scales of the neck, hinder part of the body and of the tail edged with black ; trunk with numerous oblique, alternate black and white bands converging towards the head ; lower parts marbled with blackish, or uniform pale greenish.

" β. Brownish-olive, uniform anteriorly, with the scales black-edged posteriorly ; each scale of the tail with a very distinct white, black-edged ocellus, as in *Ptyas mucosus*.

" γ. Uniform brownish black, scales of the hinder part of the body and of the tail somewhat lighter in the centre ; all the lower parts black, except the chin and throat, which are yellow."

The *first* variety is found in Bengal, Assam, the Malayan Peninsula, and Southern India (Fayrer); the *second* in Bengal (Fayrer); in the Philippine Islands and perhaps in Burmah (Günther); and the *third* is found in Borneo (Fayrer).

Günther says, "Young specimens have a much more varied coloration; they are black, with numerous white, equidistant, narrow cross-bands, descending obliquely backwards; head with four white cross-bands; one occupies the extremity of the snout, the second across the posterior frontals, the third across the crown of the head, behind the orbit; the fourth across the occiput to the angle of the mouth; the two latter bands are composed of oval spots. In a specimen from the Anamallay Mountains the belly is black, and the white bands extend across, being wider than on the back; in a second specimen, of which the locality is unknown, the belly is white, each ventral having a blackish margin."

Though this genus has a wide distribution, it is not frequently met with. It is said to be found in the Andaman and Philippine Islands, Java, Sumatra, Borneo (Günther), and in New Guinea (Duméril), Cuttack, in Bengal (Beddome), Rangoon (Fayrer). It is found in the Sunderbunds, and around Calcutta.

It is, perhaps, the most aggressive of all the Indian Thanatophidia. All the best authorities agree on this point. But it is nevertheless manageable in captivity. As its name implies, it lives, doubtless, as much as practicable, upon snakes.

For the purposes which this work is intended to subserve, it may be regarded that, with few exceptions, all hooded snakes are poisonous. Sir Joseph Fayrer has noted the dilatable neck "in *Compsosoma radiatum*, an innocent snake, the neck and much of the whole body dilates vertically when it is excited and about to strike, presenting a very remarkable appearance;" also "in the *Tropidonotus macrophthalmus*, an innocent snake, which attains a length of thirty-nine inches, according to Günther, and is found in Khasya and Sikkim up to 4000 feet. It is known by its large eye and dilatable neck" (Fayrer); the scales, Günther says, "show an arrangement very similar to that of the cobra, for which it is frequently taken. All the specimens I have seen show unmistakable signs that their captors considered it best to kill them from a distance, and to inflict a death-wound as near to the head as possible. Brown or blackish brown above, uniform or with a dorsal series of reddish brown spots; neck with an indistinct arrow-shaped mark. Anterior part of the belly with large quadrangular blackish-brown spots, posterior part and lower side of the tail more or less clouded with brown. Young specimens have indistinct square, dark spots on the back, arranged in quincunx, and a bright yellow collar broadly edged with black."

BUNGARUS FASCIATUS.

FROM LIFE REDUCED

Length 3'10". Circum 3½"

Govt. Sch. of Art Calcutta

BUNGARUS.

Günther's description of this genus is given below.

"Body rather elongate; tail comparatively short; head more or less dilated, depressed, with broad, rounded muzzle; scarcely distinct from neck, which is not dilatable. Eye small, with round pupil. Rostral shield broader than high, reaching to upper part of snout; anterior frontals half the size of the posterior; vertical five-sided; occipitals tapering behind. Nostril rather wide between two nasals. Loreal none; one præ-, two post-oculars. Seven upper labials, the third and fourth entering the orbit. Scales smooth, moderately imbricate, disposed in oblique rows, forming fifteen longitudinal series round the body; those of the vertebral series are very broad hexagonal. Ventrals between 200 and 250; anal and sub-caudals entire. Scales without apicial groove. Maxillary bone with a fang in front; a second small simple tooth at some distance behind the fang."

"The Bungarums," says Sir Joseph Fayrer, "are diurnal terrestrial snakes, but like others, they generally prefer the shade to the sunshine. They are found in the open country, in grass and low jungle, and in fields. They live in holes in the ground, sometimes down among the roots of trees at a considerable depth. They are not frequently seen in inhabited places, though they do at times find their way into huts and houses. I killed a very large one in Rangoon many years ago that got into a hut full of Dhoolie bearers at the field hospital during the last Burmese war. They feed on small animals, snakes, frogs, toads, lizards, and they are very poisonous; but owing to the shortness of their fang, which is much smaller than that of the cobra, their bite is less dangerous, and excision being more practicable, treatment may be useful and recoveries more numerous."

Bungarus fasciatus.

This species is the "Sankni," or "Bungarum Pamah" of the Coromandel Coast (Russell), "Rajsamp" of some natives. It varies in size from four to six or eight feet. Günther describes it as follows:—"The first temporal shield is scarcely larger than high ventrals 200–233; sub-caudals, 32–36. Body with alternate broad black and yellowish rings, extending across the belly; there are from twenty-five to thirty-three of these black rings round the trunk; the first is the broadest, and produced into a triangular process, the point of which rests on the vertical shield. Head black anteriorly and on the sides separated from the triangular process by a yellow V-like mark. Lower parts and throat uniform yellow." The trigonal shape of its body with sharp dorsal ridge and declining sides are noted by Russell. "The hexagonal vertebral shield, and hard, blunt, and almost bony end of tail, are very strongly marked."

"The *Bungarus fasciatus,*" says Sir Joseph Fayrer, "is tolerably common in Bengal and in Southern India, as well as Burmah, and it is also known in the North-West, where it is sometimes called 'Koclia Krait.' Its bite is very dangerous, but the police returns do not show that it causes many deaths; probably because it is not so much in the way of being met with as the cobra or krait. Its fangs are relatively to those of the cobra very small, and its bite in dogs causes death much slower than the cobra's bite. It is much less valued by the snake-men than the cobra, as it does not erect its head, nor is it amenable to their tuition. Dogs bitten by *Bungarus fasciatus* died at various periods from four hours twenty-eight minutes to ten days."

Plate 4

GALLOPHIS MACLELLANDII.

FROM NATURE. IND MUS (REDUCED)

Length 1' 2½". Circum ⅝

Drawn by Harrish Chunder Khan, Student

BUNGARUS CŒRULEUS.

FROM LIFE. (REDUCED.)

Length 2' 6". Circum. 1¾"

Drawn by Annoda Prosad Bagchee, Student

Govt. Sch. of Art, Calcutta.

BUNGARUS CÆRULEUS.

This species is the krait of India. It is the "Gedi Paragoodoo" of Russell; the "Dhomun Chiti" (Bengal). Günther describes this snake as follows :—"The first temporal shield is considerally longer than high. Ventrals, 201–221; sub-caudals, 38–56. Lower parts uniform white; upper parts bluish or brownish-black, uniform, or with more or less numerous very narrow white cross streaks, not quite as broad as a scale, and generally radiating from a white vertebral spot. No collar."

Varieties.—"α. Upper parts uniform blackish-brown; *B. lividus*, Cautor from Assam. In young specimens the head is white, with a black line between the occipitals.

"β. A vertebral series of equi-distant white spots, from which narrow transverse streaks proceed.

"γ. Upper parts with narrow white streaks arranged in pairs: *B. arcuatus*, Dum. and Bib."

It varies in size from two feet to four feet and a half. The fangs are smaller than those of the cobra. I have seen it in the North-West, Rajputana, Guzerat, Deccan, and Madras. It is found in fields, huts, houses, in bookcases, ledges of windows, and venetians. Fayrer mentions an instance "where, after a night's dâk in a palanquin, a lady, in taking out her things on arriving at her destination, found a krait coiled up under her pillow; it had been her travelling companion all night." It is often mistaken for the *Lycodon aulicus*, which is an innocent snake. In the krait, the hexagonal scales on back, and its fangs are sufficient to distinguish it from the *Lycodon aulicus*.

Callophis Macclellandia.

This species of callophis is described by Günther as follows :—"Upper labials, seven; temporals, small, 1+1+1; anal bifid. Head and neck black above, with a yellow cross band behind the eyes. Body and tail reddish-brown, generally with a black vertebral line from the nape to the tip of the tail. Belly yellowish, with black cross-bands or quadrangular black spots."

Varieties.—"*a.* Belly with uninterrupted black cross-bands, alternately limited to the belly, or extending up the sides of the body, so as to cover scales of the four outer rows, and give the appearance of a lateral series of large black spots. The three last cross-bands of the trunk form complete rings crossing the vertebral line; tail with three other black rings. This specimen is twenty-six and one-third inches long; tail, two and one-third inches; ventrals, 218; sub-caudals, 28.

"β. Belly with quadrangular black spots, rather irregularly disposed, and not extending up the sides. Tail without black rings. This specimen is eighteen inches long; tail, one and a half inch; ventrals, 224; sub-caudals, 25.

"γ. The cross-bands reach entirely across the back, forming rings, from twenty-two to twenty-eight in number; no black vertebral line, which, however, is indicated by isolated small spots. Ventrals, 198–218; sub-caudals, 27–34. Varieties α and β are from Nepaul and Darjeeling; γ from Assam."

Plate 5

DABOIA RUSSELLI.

FROM LIFE. (REDUCED)

Length 3'8". Circum. 5".

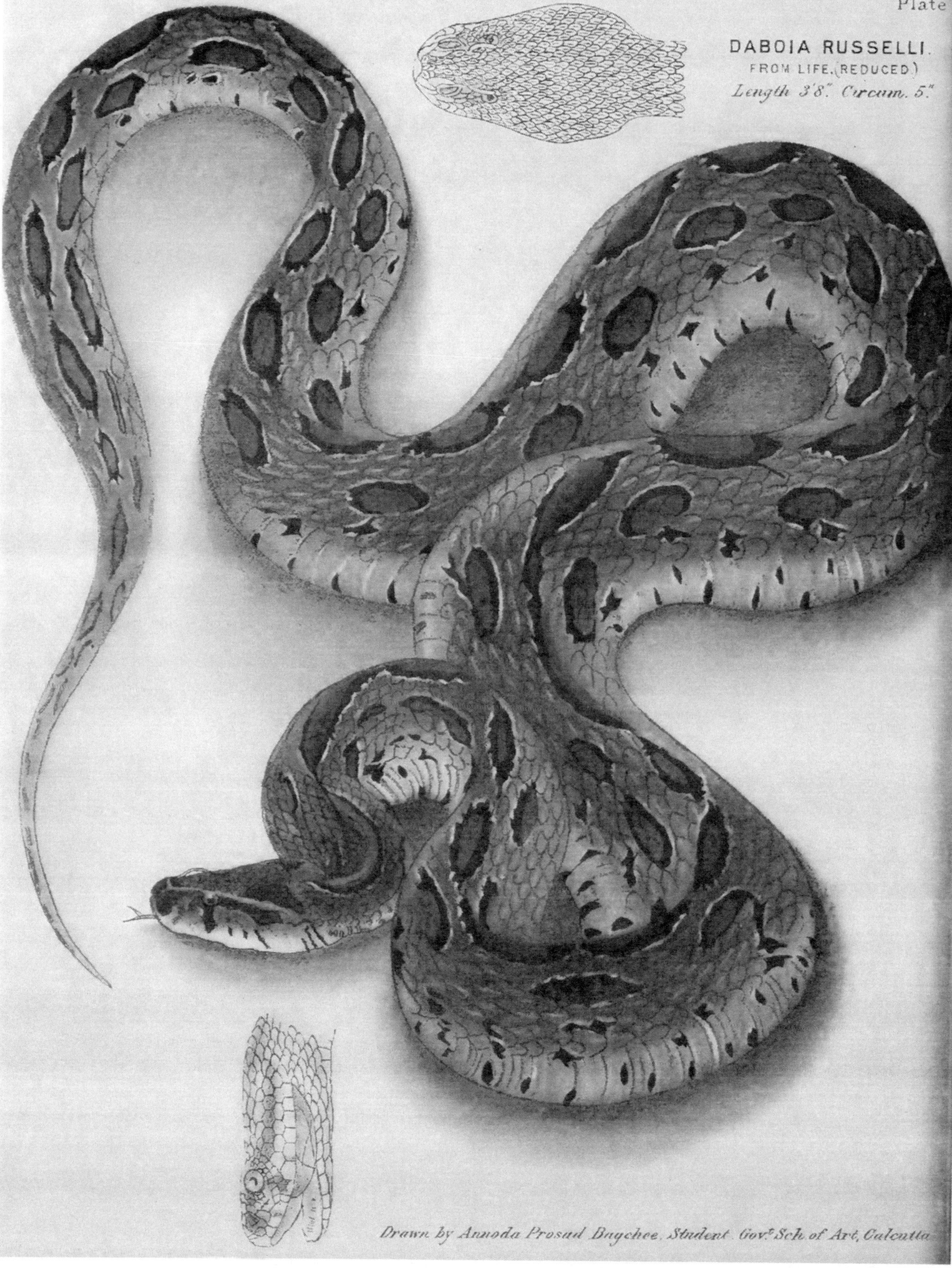

Drawn by Annoda Prosad Bagchee. Student. Govt. Sch. of Art, Calcutta.

DABOIA.

There is only one species of this genus—the Daboia Russellii, Russell's Viper, Tic-polonga, or Daboia elegans, or Chain Viper, Uloo Bora in and around Calcutta (Fayrer); in Bengal, Jessur, Siah-chunder Amaiter (Fayrer). Günther's description of this viper is as follows :—" Greyish" (light chocolate colour) " brown, with three series of large black, white-edged rings, those of the middle series ovate, those of the outer circular; sometimes very small black, white-edged ocelli are scattered between the rings. A yellow line on each side of the upper surface of the head, the two lines convergent on the snout. Rostral and labial shields yellow, with brown margins; a sub-triangular brown, black-edged spot below the eye. Belly uniform yellowish, or marbled with brownish; generally more or less numerous semicircular brown spots on the hinder margins of the ventral shields. Ventrals, 163–170; sub-caudals, 45–60."

I have seen it in Rajputana and Guzerat. It is said to prevail in most parts of India. Fayrer says "it is probably found all over the plains of India, as well as in the hills." In Kulu it has been observed 5000 feet high, and in Kashmir 6000 feet high, but generally not higher than from 2000 to 4000 feet. According to Stoliczka, it is fond of basking in sunny places.

"It is the 'Tic-polonga' of Ceylon, and is justly dreaded there as a very deadly snake. Dr. Russell describes it in his work on Indian snakes under the name of 'Katuka Rekula Poda.' He says it is not as venomous as the cobra. My experiments incline me to agree with Dr. Russell, and to give it, at all events, a place next to the cobra. Fowls bitten by this snake expired in from thirty-five seconds to several minutes; dogs in from seven minutes to several hours; a cat in fifty-seven minutes; a horse in eleven and a half hours. Death was not in any case so rapid as after the cobra bite; but, though slower in its action, the poison seemed just as deadly. The blood usually remains fluid after death from the poison of the Daboia (the human subject perhaps being excepted); whereas after cobra poisoning it generally coagulates firmly on being removed from the heart and great vessels. The Daboia is nocturnal in its habits; in confinement it is sluggish, and does not readily strike, unless roused and irritated, when it bites with great force and determination. When disturbed it hisses fiercely, and when it strikes, does so with great vigour. Its long, movable fangs are very prominent objects, and with them it is capable of inflicting a very deep as well as poisoned wound. The markings on its body are very beautiful, and justify the synonym, *V. elegans.* It lives on small animals, such as rats, mice, and frogs. My snake-man says it will go into water. It is, however, terrestrial in its habits. (It climbs trees in Ceylon.—*Tennant*). Its loud hissing when disturbed is calculated to warn those who come within its dangerous proximity. Though so deadly, it does not appear by the returns to cause many deaths; but this may be owing to the fact that the natives seldom know, often do not see, the snake that has inflicted the fatal wound. It is much less known, and its misdeeds are therefore doubtless often ascribed to the cobra. In the official returns of deaths from snake bites, a large number are attributed to snakes unknown. If the real offender could be detected, it is probable that the *Daboia* would have a more prominent place than it occupies at present."—(*Fayrer.*) The adult varies in length from three to four feet or so.

Plate 6.

ECHIS CARINATA.

Life Size.

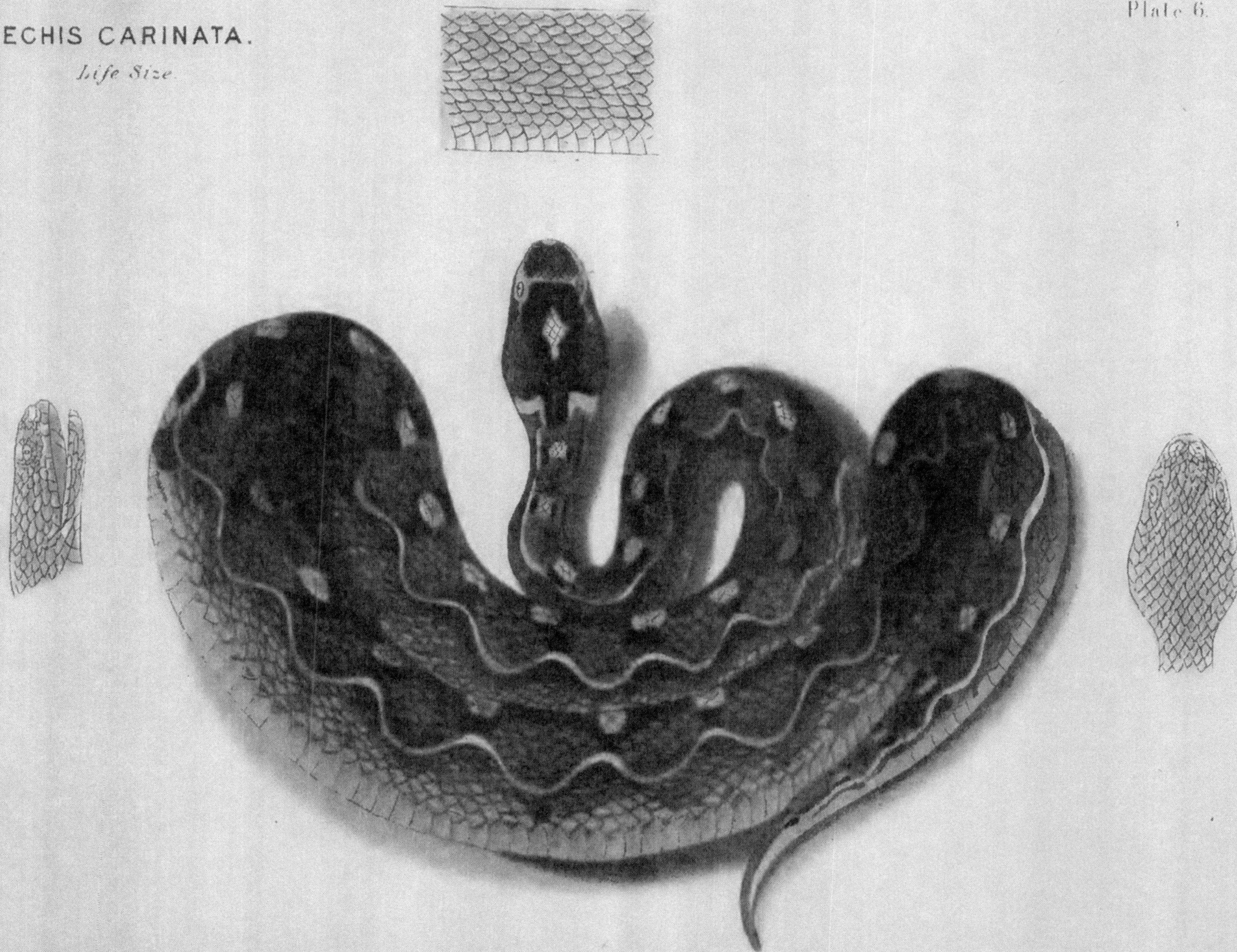

Drawn by Annoda Prosod Bagchee, Student

Govt. Sch. of Art, Calcutta

ECHIS.

Echis carinata.

Of the genus *Echis*, the *Echis carinata* is the only Indian species. It prevails in the North-West Provinces, Punjab, Rajputana, Central India, Sind, and in some parts of the Madras Presidency. About Delhi its indigenous name is "Afäe" (Fayrer). By Russell it is figured under the name of "Horatta Pam." In Sind it is known as the "Kuppur." The genus is described by Günther as follows:—"Head covered with keeled scales; a pair of very small frontals behind the rostral shield. Nostril small, round, directed upwards, situated in a large nasal shield, which is subdivided behind the nostril. Sides of the head covered with keeled scales, two series of which are between the eye and the low upper labials. Scales much imbricate, strongly keeled, in from twenty-five to twenty-nine series; those in the lateral series have their tips directed obliquely downwards." "With these they make the rustling sound" (Fayrer). "Sub-caudals one-rowed." The species *Echis carinata* is described by Günther as follows:—"Brown or brownish grey, with a series of sub-quadrangular or ovate whitish spots, edged with blackish brown; a sub-semicircular whitish band on each side of each of the dorsal spots, enclosing a round, dark brown lateral spot. A pair of oblong brown, black edged spots on the crown of the head, convergent anteriorly; a brown spot below, and an oblique broad streak behind the eye. Belly whitish, with more or less numerous round brown specks. Ventrals, 149–154; sub-caudals, 21–26."

"The Echis," says Sir Joseph Fayrer, "is fierce and aggressive. It is always on the defensive, ready to attack; it throws itself into a double coil, the folds of which are in perpetual motion, and as they rub against each other, they make a loud rustling sound, very like hissing. This sound is produced by the three or four outer rows of carinated scales, which are very prominent, and point downwards at a different angle to the rest; their friction against each other causes the sound. This little viper does not, I think, hiss at all. Its fangs are very long and mobile, like those of the *Daboia*. Its eye has a peculiarly vicious appearance. . . . . It is a small viper; a specimen from the Indian Museum is twenty-two and a half inches in length and about three in circumference, though no doubt it has somewhat shrunk by the action of the spirit. . . . . It is very active, and can dart a considerable distance—a foot or more—to strike its prey: it is by far the most active and aggressive poisonous snake I have seen."

Plate 7

TRIMERESURUS CARINATUS

Specimen in Indian Museum

Length 3' Circum 4

Drawn by ... Chunder Khan, Student | *Govt. Sch. of Art Calcutta*

TRIMERESURUS CARINATUS.

One of the Crotalidæ or Pit Vipers, found in Bengal, Sikkim, and sub-Himalaya and Burmah. Günther's description is as follows:—"The second upper labial shield forms the front part of the facial pit. Scales in from twenty-three to twenty-five rows; those on the crown of the head and on the temples small, strongly carinated. Ventrals, 164–169; sub-caudals, 34–60. Grass green above, tail yellowish green; a more or less distinct yellowish line runs along the outer series of scales, and is sometimes absent. Lower parts greenish white. The general colour is usually green; sometimes there are large blackish spots on the sides; the lateral line is either well developed, white margined, with coral red below, or it is absent. Tail pale, ruddy above, usually equal to one-sixth the total length."

Plate 8

TRIMERESURUS ANAMALLENSIS

TRIMERESURUS ERYTHRURUS

Length including Tail 2' 2"

Tail 3¼

Girth of body 2"

Do. of neck ¾

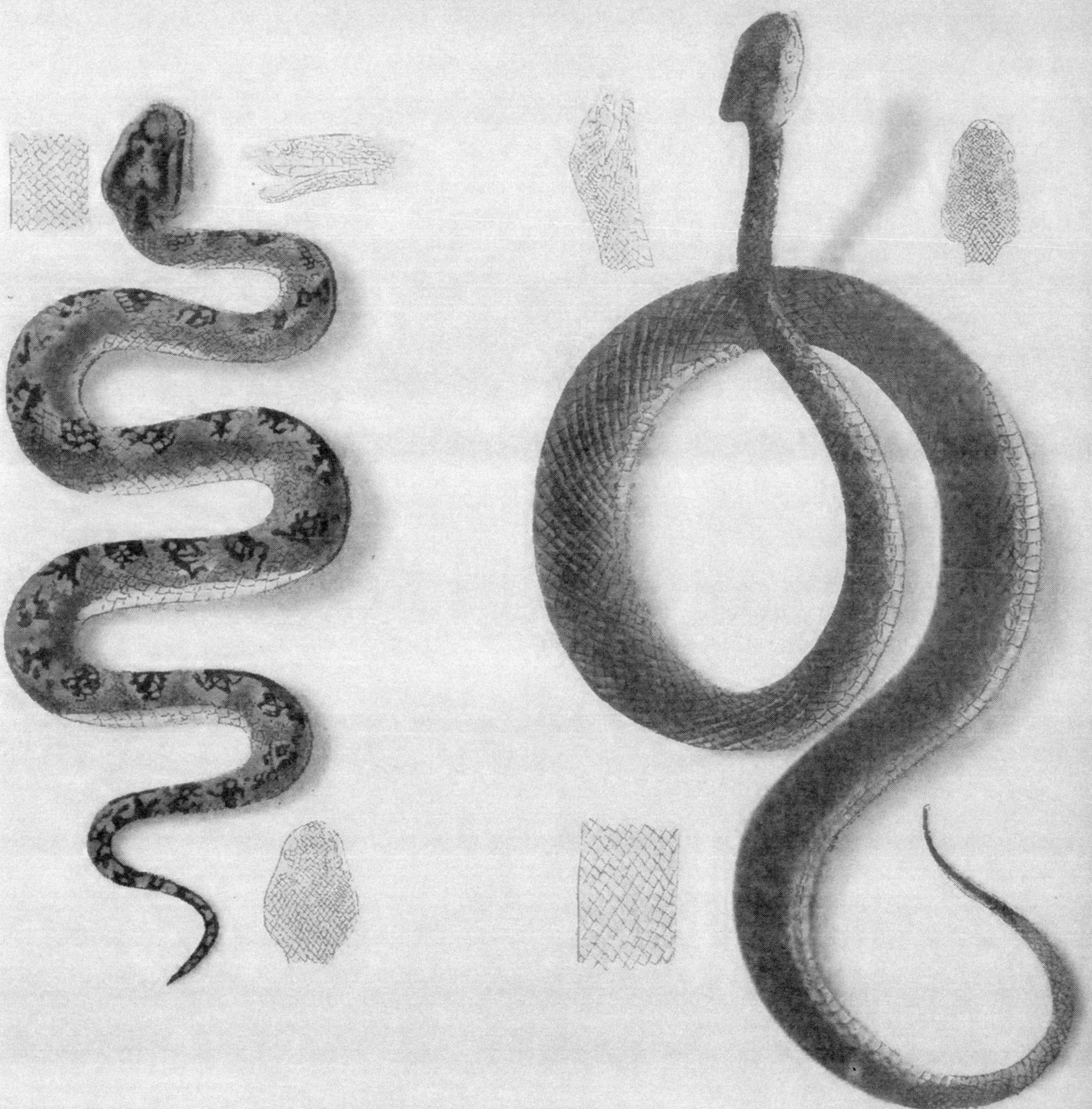

Drawn by Annoda Prasad Bagchee *Students* *Drawn by Nityananda Dey*

Govt. Sch. of Art Calcutta

TRIMERESURUS ANAMALLENSIS.

The description of this snake by Günther is as follows:—"The second upper labial shield forms the front part of the facial pit, generally a small shield between the supra-nasals. Scales on the head and on the body more or less distinctly keeled, in twenty-one series. Ventrals, 148–158; sub-caudals, 51–55. Ground colour generally yellowish green, with a dorsal series of large rhombic black spots, each spot subdivided by or variegated with yellow. Upper side of the head marbled with black in adult specimens, uniform greenish in young ones; a black or brown band runs from the back edge of the eye to the angle of the mouth; supra-ciliary, with one or two black cross streaks. Belly yellowish green, with numerous yellow and green spots along its side. Tail black, with yellow and green spots. Young specimens may be recognised by the dark temple streak; but nearly all the other markings are very indistinct, and the ground colour is a reddish olive; tail with white extremity.

"A specimen received with others from the same locality has a brownish purple ground colour, with a dorsal series of brown spots; belly marbled with purple; tail black, with irregular greenish rings, and with some indistinct small yellowish spots. This specimen also has the supra-ciliary divided into two; but, nevertheless, we consider it merely a variety of about a dozen specimens from the Anamally Mountains; the largest is twenty-four inches long, tail measuring three and a half inches."

Of three specimens forwarded by Dr. Shortt, of Madras, to Sir Joseph Fayrer, one was nineteen inches long, one inch and three-quarters in girth, tail measuring two inches and three-quarters; a second was twenty-seven inches long, and two inches and three-quarters in girth, tail being three inches and a half; whilst a third one, which had become greatly decomposed, was also of same length and girth as the second snake. All the three had the supra-ciliary divided into two shields as noted by Günther.

Trimeresurus Erythrurus.

"Dr. Stoliczka says that its head is elongately oval, and more depressed than either *T. carinatus* or *T. gramineus*. The lips and chin are white, the lateral line is white, bordered with purple, or greenish below. Colour grass green, lighter on the sides and belly. Günther says that old females do not show either the white lips or line. In this species there is not generally an azygos shield between the supra-nasals, but Dr. Stoliczka says that there is sometimes a small azygos shield. The scales on the body are strongly carinated, in twenty-one to twenty-three series. It is said by Günther to grow to the length of thirty-three inches, and to be found in the Delta of the Ganges. Dr. Stoliczka found it common in the limestone hills about Moulmein, in Penang and Java." (Fayrer). According to Ball and Rink it is also found in the Nicobars.

TRIMERESURUS MONTICOLA.
FROM LIFE. (REDUCED)

Length 2'9"
Circum 3½"
Tail 3"

TRIMERESURUS ANDERSONII.
FROM LIFE. IND. MUS. (REDUCED)

Length 1'9"
Circum 2"
Tail 2¾"

Drawn by Hurrish Chunder Khan, Student.

Govt. Sch. of Art, Calcutta.

TRIMERESURUS MONTICOLA.

" The second upper labial forms the front of the pit. There are two small shields behind the nostril, sometimes a small azygos shield below this. The scales on the head are smooth, those on the body slightly carinated. There are twenty-three series. Ventrals 137–141; sub-caudals 41. The supra-ciliaries are very large. The coloration varies. In one specimen it is pale brown, with a vertebral row of large, square, dark brown blotches. Along the sides a row of small dark spots; a pale temple-streak. Belly dark mottled. The larger male specimen, which is also from Darjeeling, is of a dark brown or almost blackish-ash colour, with the rhomboid patches along the vertebræ. There is a peculiar mark in the middle of the neck like a U, which is of a yellowish or whitish colour." (Fayrer.) It is found in the sub-Himalaya, the Darjeeling, Sikkim, Nepaul, and Khasya Hills; and in the Neilgherries and Anamally Mountains in Southern India.

Trimeresurus Andersonii.

" Mr. Theobald has named what he considers a new species after Dr. Anderson, the Curator of the Indian Museum. It is described in his 'Catalogue of the Asiatic Society's (now Indian) Museum,' pp. 75 to 76. It has 25 rows of carinated scales, 182 ventrals, and 56 sub-caudals in one specimen, and 71 in the other. The second upper labial forms the anterior margin of the præ-orbital pit; supra-nasals separated by an azygos shield. The colour above and below is a uniform rich brown. Belly and sides marked conspicuously with white spots. Found in Assam. A second individual, named by Mr. Theobald in the same Catalogue as *T. obscurus,* has the back of a uniform brown, sides green, spotted and mottled. Belly greenish white, brown barred and spotted, supra-ciliaries well defined. But it is very doubtful if this be distinct from *T. Andersonii.* The length of the Museum specimen is twenty inches, of which the tail is two inches and three-quarters. The girth is one inch and five-eighths." (Fayrer.)

Plate 10

TRIMERESURUS STRICATUS.
SPECIMEN IN IND MUS.
Length 1' 2½". Circum 1¼

HALYS HIMALAYANUS.
SPECIMEN IN IND. MUS.
Length 1' 11". Circum 2¼".

Drawn by Hurrish Chunder Khan, Student.

Gov^t Sch. of Art, Calcutta

TRIMERESURUS STRIGATUS.

"The shield forming the front part of the facial pit is separate from the second upper labial. Supra-ciliary shield narrow; no large shields behind the rostral. The whole upper surface of the head is covered with small, nearly smooth scales. Nine or ten upper labials, becoming smaller in size behind. Scales distinctly keeled, in twenty-one series. Ventrals 136–142; sub-caudals 31–40. Tail but slightly prehensile, terminating in a short cervical scale." (Günther.)

Sir Joseph Fayrer says—"A specimen in the Indian Museum measures fourteen inches and a half; girth one inch and a quarter; it is brown, with a line of darker coloured, irregular vertebral spots. It has a horseshoe-shaped whitish mark on the neck. There is a triangular dark spot below the eye and loreal pit, and a dark brown band leading from the eye to the neck. The lower jaw and belly marked with black spots. The end of the tail terminates in a scale; in young specimens it is white." It is found on the Neilgherries, Anamallies, and Deccan. It does not measure more than nineteen inches.

Halys Himalayanus.

Günther describes the snake as follows:—"Snout of moderate length, broader than long, with the nose rather protruding. Rostral shield oblique, higher than broad; frontals well developed, not broken up into smaller shields. The anterior frontals short, transversely produced, and tapering on the sides; both taken together form a sort of crescent. Posterior frontals large, somewhat pointed in front, and rounded behind. Vertical and supra-ciliaries as usual in this genus; occipitals rather small, rounded. Five upper labials, a sixth and seventh being confluent with the temporals; the second is small, not entering the margin of the facial pit; the third enters the orbit. There is a series of three large temporal shields, the two hinder of which form a portion of the lip; the space between these temporals and the occipital is covered with small scales. Body of moderate length, rounded; its middle is covered with twenty-three series of strongly keeled scales. Ventrals 162–166; anal entire; sub-caudals 43–51. The tail terminates in a long spine. Dark brown, with large band-like spots across the back; these spots are very indistinct, scarcely differing from the ground colour, and becoming visible only by their black edges; belly almost entirely black, marbled with yellowish. A broad blackish brown band runs from the eye along the series of temporal shields to the angle of the mouth; it has a narrow black and white edge above and below, and is better defined in the young individual than in the old one. Lower labials marbled with yellowish and blackish."

Dr. Stoliczka says—"Especially between 5000 and 8000 feet, but on the Hatu Mountain near Kotegurh, and about Serahan, I observed it as high as 10,000 feet. It feeds principally on mice. . . . . The upper ground colour of this snake varies from brownish-green to almost brownish-black, but generally with some lighter spots, bands or marblings, and that of the lower part is of a greenish-yellow purple tinge, the purplish colour sometimes predominating, especially on the sub-caudals; the whole of the lower side is more or less strongly marbled with greenish black; rarely is the under side nearly all black, but the chin is always yellowish. The upper labials are yellowish white, and in continuation of this colour, there is in younger specimens a very conspicuous whitish lateral band occupying the base of the ventrals, and the adjoining row of scales. In old specimens this lateral band is only indicated on the throat, becoming obsolete on the body. . . . . All the specimens which I examined had only twenty-one series of scales. One nearly full grown, from the neighbourhood of Kotegurh (north-east of Simla) measures twenty-five inches and a quarter, of which the tail is three and a quarter, terminating with a very small single sub-caudal scale. Ventrals 160; sub-caudals 42." It is "very common over the north-west Himalayas." (Fayrer.) It is "met with on the paths generally after rains, and in shady places between overhanging forest trees." (Stoliczka.)

Plate II

PELAMIS BICOLOR

From Pooru

Length 1' 2" Circum 1½

HYPNALE NEPA (CARAWALA)

From a drawing of Dr. Shortts

Madras.

Drawn by Hurrish Chunder Khan, Student
Govt. Sch of Art, Calcutta

Copied by Hurrish Chunder Khan, from
an original drawing by C. Abbov Madras

HYPNALE NEPA (CARAWILLA).

This snake is found in Malabar, Anamallay Mountains, and Ceylon. According to Günther the largest size is nineteen inches, the tail accounting for two and a half inches. Günther describes it as follows :—"Head broad, triangular; snout covered with numerous small shields above, the crown of the head being normally shielded. Body of moderate length, with keeled scales in seventeen rows. Tail rather short, not prehensile, terminating in a short cervical scale. Sub-caudals two-rowed **. Ventrals 140–152, sub-caudals 31–45 ***. Brown or grey, or reddish olive, with a double dorsal series of brown or black spots; the spots of both sides sometimes confluent into cross-bands. Sides and belly finely marbled and dotted with brown or black. Upper lip brown or black, well marked by a darker line running from behind the eye to the angle of the mouth; a more or less distinct white or whitish temporal streak above the dark line, sometimes continued along the side of the neck, with an interrupted brown band above and below it. Chin and throat blackish and brownish, variegated with yellow or grey. Sometimes specimens occur of a more uniform coloration; the dorsal spots on each side of the throat are the most constant markings, as described. All these varieties may be seen in the fœtus taken out of the same female **. The carawilla is much dreaded, although its bite is but exceptionally fatal to man, and in such cases death does not occur before the lapse of some days." Sir Joseph Fayrer says that he has "had no opportunity of testing by experiment the properties of this snake."

SEA SNAKES.

Pelamis bicolor.

Günther's description is as follows :—" Head flat, with very long, spatulate snout ; neck rather stout ; body of moderate length. Nasal shields contiguous, longer than broad, pierced by the nostril posteriorly ; only one pair of frontals. Scales not imbricate, not polished, tubercular or concave. Ventral shields none, or very narrow. Lower jaw without notch in front **. Two or three post-orbitals. Neck surrounded by from forty-five to fifty-one longitudinal series of scales. From 378 to 440 scales in a lateral longitudinal series between the angle of the mouth and the vent. Coloration variable."

Varieties :—" *a*. Colour, black above ; sides and belly uniform brownish olive ; tail with black spots.

" *β*. Back black ; belly and sides brown ; separated by a black and yellow band. Large spots posteriorly.

" *γ*. Black of back narrow, becomes sinuous behind middle of the body ; posteriorly a dorsal series of rhombic confluent spots. Sides and belly with an irregular series of rounded black or brown spots.

" *δ*. Yellow, with about fifty brown, black-edged cross-bands, extending nearly to the belly, which is crossed by narrow vertical brownish-black streaks, alternating with the dorsal bands. Some of the dorsal bands are confluent, forming a zigzag band. Head yellow, variegated with black."

This is the only species of the genus Pelamis. It has a wide distribution—wider indeed than that of any other known salt-water snake. It abounds in the Bay of Bengal, and in " all the Eastern seas." A specimen sent by Mr. Stewart, of Pooree, to Sir Joseph Fayrer, is " twelve and a half inches long, and is uniform black above, the sides and the belly being of a bright gamboge yellow, tail with black spots, separated by a well-defined line. It is described as being very poisonous, and killed a fowl rapidly."

Plate 12

VALAKADYEN

ENHYDRINA BENGALENSIS

FROM LIFE AND MUS. REDUCED

Length 31" Greum 4

Drawn by Hurrish Chunder Khan, Student. *Govt. Sch. of Art, Calcutta.*

ENHYDRINA BENGALENSIS.

Russell's description of this species of Enhydrina is given below:—"Head rather short, of moderate width; neck and body moderately elongate. Rostral shield very small, lobuliform, its projecting point fitting into a corresponding cavity of the lower jaw; the fourth upper labial shield below the eye; mental shield very narrow and long, situated in a groove; anterior lower labials much elongate; throat covered with scales, without shields. One post-ocular, sometimes divided into two. Neck surrounded by forty-eight series of scales. Scales scarcely imbricate, hexagonal, each provided with a short keel; ventral shields not, or but little, different from the scales of the adjoining series; they are 284–314 in number. Terminal scale of the tail rather large. The young has broad black rhombic bands across the back, which become fainter with age, and finally disappear entirely."

"The fang of Enhydrina," says Sir Joseph Fayrer, "is short, but well marked; the groove is open part of its length, but not throughout. The body is somewhat compressed, the belly carinate; the tail flat and compressed, almost like a fish's fin; the nostrils vertical; the eyes small ***. One (Enhydrina) was made to close its jaws on a fowl, and it killed it in seven minutes. Some hours after its death its jaws were forcibly closed on a fowl's thigh, and the bird died in four hours. The poison is evidently very virulent." According to Fayrer it measures from thirty-six to forty-eight inches. It is common in the tidal waters of the Sunderbunds and in the Bay of Bengal.

Plate 13

PLATURUS FISCHERI.

FROM NATURE IND. MUS. REDUCED.

Length including tail	4′ 0″
Tail	4½″
Girth of body	4½″
Girth of neck	2¾″

Drawn by Behary Lall Das, Student — *Gov^t. Sch. of Art, Calcutta*

PLATURUS FISCHERI.

Günther describes this species as follows :—

"No azygos shield between the posterior frontals, scales of the front part of the trunk in nineteen longitudinal series ; ventral shields 232–241. Trunk surrounded by from thirty-three to thirty-six black rings, which are broader than the interspaces. A black band crosses the occiput and extends forward over the vertical plate and over the lower jaw, but, generally, it is not confluent with the next following ring. The upper part of the snout yellow ; upper labials black."

Dr. John Anderson, the distinguished Director of the Indian Museum, Calcutta, furnished Sir Joseph Fayrer with the following description of what he considered to be a specimen of *P. Fischeri* in the Museum :—

"The specimen which I provisionally refer to this species has nineteen rows of smooth scales round the fore part of the trunk, in longitudinal series, and 235 ventrals. There is no azygos shield between the posterior frontals, and in all of these characters it agrees with this species. But on comparing the head with Günther's drawing, I find that the anterior frontals in my specimen differ from it, in being long and pointed anteriorly, and considerably larger than the posterior pair, and in the vertical being proportionally larger than in *P. Fischeri,* and the occipitals larger and more pointed. It has one præ-, and two post-oculars, and the third and fourth labials are below the eye. Two pairs of large chin-shields, the posterior shields with a large scale between their posterior extremities. It also differs from *P. Fischeri* in having fifty-six black rings round the trunk instead of thirty-six, but I do not attach much importance to this, as *P. scutatus* shows about an equal variation ; but at the same time, Günther's statement that his eight specimens show the same assemblage of characters as laid down in his description, and the occurrence of fifty-six rings in my specimen, suggest that their multiplicity is either due to greater age (it measures forty-nine inches in length) or to variation. The head too is wholly black, with the exception of a yellow band from the posterior margin of one eye to the other. The upper surface is olive green, and the sides and belly rich dark gamboge yellow, and the fifty-six rings are intensely bluish-black, and the scales generally have a very bright shining lustre. It was from Tolly's Nullah, a tidal stream near Calcutta. The largest of Günther's eight specimens measured thirty inches."

HYDROPHIS JERDONII.

FROM NATURE. IND. MUS. (REDUCED)

Length including tail 3′ 0″
Tail 3½″
Girth of body 2″

Plate 14

Drawn by Nityananda Day. Student.

Govt. Sch. of Art, Calcutta

HYDROPHIS JERDONII.

Dr. Anderson describes this species as follows :—

"Head short, with the snout declivous and rather pointed; body of moderate length. Frontal shields small, not much larger than præocular; one post-ocular; five upper labial shields, the third and fourth of which enter the orbit, the last below the post-ocular; two or three large temporals on the side of each occipital, the anterior of which enters the labial margin behind the fifth labial shield. Two pairs of chin-shields, in contact with one another. Scales imbricate, large, higher than long, with apex slightly truncated; each scale with a strong keel; they are disposed in fifteen or seventeen series round the neck, and in nineteen or twenty-one in the middle of the body. Ventral shields distinct, but not twice as large as the scales of the adjoining series, bituberculate 235–238 in number. Anal shields small; terminal scale of the tail large. A series of seven simple teeth behind the grooved fang in front. Trunk with from thirty-four to thirty-eight black cross-bands, broadest on the back and extending to the belly in young and half-grown specimens."

Plate 15.

HYDROPHIS ROBUSTA.

FROM NATURE IND MUS REDUCED

Length including tail 5' 10½"
Tail. 6"
Girth of body. 4½"

Drawn by Hurrish Chunder Khan, Student

Govt. Sch. of Art Calcutta

HYDROPHIS ROBUSTA.

"Head of moderate size and width; neck and body not elongate. Two or three upper labials below the orbit; one post-ocular; anterior temporal shield large; two pairs of chin-shields, which are in contact with one another. Thirty-one series of scales round the neck. Scales slightly imbricate, each with a subcentral tubercle; those on the highest part of the body are rounded or subtruncated behind, as high as long. Ventrals twice or thrice as broad as the scales of the adjoining series, smooth, 310 in number. Terminal scale of the tail rather large. Trunk with thirty-five narrow, distant, black rings, extending round the belly, sometimes interrupted on the side and dilated on the back; head without markings in the adult; throat and belly whitish. This snake, of which we have examined two adult examples, six feet long, is found on the coast of the mainland of India, as well as in the Archipelago. It has been confounded with other species by all the previous herpetologists. The figure given by Fischer is very recognisable."

HYDROPHIS GRASSICOLLIS.

FROM NATURE. IND. MUS. REDUCED.

Length including tail	4'3"
Tail	4"
Girth of body	3
Girth of neck	2.

Drawn by Nityanunda Day, Student. *Govt Sch of Art Calcutta*

HYDROPHIS CRASSICOLLIS (N.S) ANDERSON.

"Head hardly distinct from neck. Neck and body of nearly equal girth throughout. Round neck, 2″ 2‴; round middle of body, 2″ 9‴. Body elongated; thirty-four series of scales round the neck; forty round the middle of the body; scales almost smooth on the neck and anterior third of the body; two feeble keel-like tubercles, one before the other, very obscure, but more strongly developed on the two posterior thirds; ventrals twice the size of the adjoining scales, quite smooth, broken up here and there on the posterior five-eighths of the body. Two pairs of anal-shields, the central pair of moderate size, elongated; the external pair very large. The vertical is pointedly linguate. One præ-, and two post-oculars. The third, fourth, and fifth labials enter the orbit on one side, but only the third and the fourth on the opposite side; the fifth being transversely divided into two shields, which do not reach quite as high as the orbital margin. Two pairs of large chin-shields, the anterior pair quadrangular and the posterior pair rather elongated; olive-yellow above, yellowish on the scales and under surface; sixty-two broad black bands on the back contracting to a point on the sides, but prolonged very indistinctly on to them and the ventral aspect, where they expand as a large blackish spot. Near the tail the dorsal bands become connected together, and their continuations on the ventral aspect follow a similar arrangement. Six black rings on the tail, confluent below; the latter third entirely black. Hooghly, below Calcutta. Length (total) 4 feet, 5″ 6‴, tail 4″ 3‴. The peculiarity of this species is its elongated body, the uniform breadth which it preserves throughout its length and the enlarged and smooth ventrals." It is found in the tidal streams near Calcutta (Fayrer).

HYDROPHIS CYANOCINTA.

FROM NATURE. IND. MUS. (REDUCED)

Length including tail	5' 9"
Tail	6"
Girth of body	4½"

Plate 17

Drawn by Behari Lal Dass, Student — *Govt. Sch. of Art, Calcutta*

HYDROPHIS CYANOCINCTA.

"Head of moderate size and width; neck and body rather elongate; generally two labial shields below the eye; two post-oculars (exceptionally confluent into one); two or more temporal-shields on the side of each occipital; two pairs of chin-shields, the anterior of which are in contact with each other; twenty-nine to thirty-three series of scales round the neck. Scales slightly imbricate, rhombic, faintly keeled; three on the highest part of the body, rather longer than high. Ventrals, 320–360—406–426, twice or thrice as large as the scales of the adjoining series; almost all are entire, not longitudinally divided, and bitubercular; four anal-shields, the outer of which are larger than the inner; terminal scale of the tail rather small or of moderate size. Greenish-olive on the back, yellowish on the sides and belly; trunk with from fifty to seventy-five black cross-bands, which are broadest on the back and broader than the interspaces of the ground colour; they are narrower on the sides, sometimes disappearing altogether with age on the sides and belly, or visible only as irregular spots on the ventral shields. In young and half-grown specimens they surround the body entirely, and are sometimes joined by a black band running along the whole line of the ventral shields. The head is greenish-olive above and yellowish on the sides; in the young, black variegated with yellow, the yellow colour sometimes forming a frontal and temporal band. This is one of the commonest sea-snakes, occurring on the coasts of Ceylon, Madras, in the Bay of Bengal, in the East Indian Archipelago, and in the seas of China and Japan. It attains to a length of more than six feet. Old males have a remarkably thick and rounded tail."

Plate 18

HYDROPHIS STUARTII. (ANDERSON).
FROM NATURE POOREE ORISSA (REDUCED)
Length including tail 2' 11" *Length of Tail 3"*
Girth of Body 3½" *Girth of Neck 1¾"*

HYDROPHIS CURTA
SPECIMEN IN IND MU.
Length 1' 4½" Circum 2"

Drawn by Annoda Prosad Bagchee. *Students. Govt. School of Art Calcutta.* *Drawn by Hurrish Chunder Khan.*

HYDROPHIS STEWARTII (N.S.), ANDERSON.

"The neck moderately long and slender, and the head rather short and not much broader than the neck. The remainder of the body very much compressed. Rostral considerably broader than high. The nasals as broad posteriorly as they are long. The third and fourth labials enter the orbit, the former not being in contact with the nasal. Three temporals, the anterior the largest. Two post-oculars. Vertical much pointed behind; occipitals long and narrow. Two almost quadrangular chin-shields in contact with each other. Thirty-three rows of scales round the neck. The scales hexagonal, not imbricate, with a feeble central tubercle. Ventrals 387, smooth. The first forty on the neck about four times as large as the adjoining scales, those behind them being small and narrow as they are traced backwards, and hardly discernible on the last six inches of the trunk. Two pairs of small scale-like anals. Tail broad, markedly dilating from its root. Lips yellowish. Upper surface of head and upper surface of neck and trunk greenish olive. Under surface of head and sides and under surface of neck and trunk salmon coloured. Fifty-seven very obscure darker olive, almost black bars on the dorsal area of the neck and compressed portion, but not extending on to the light coloured sides. The tail greenish olive, mottled, and tipped with black.

"Length, 38″ 3‴, of which the tail constitutes 2″ 8‴. Girth round neck, two inches behind head, 2″ 5‴. Greatest depth of body, five inches before the tail, 1″ 8‴. Greatest thickness at that point, 0″ 3‴. Thickness at ventral margin at the same situation, 0″ 2‴. Snout to occiput, 0″ 11‴. Breadth across angle of mouth, 0″ 7‴. Locality—Pooree, Cuttack."

Hydrophis Curta.

"Head short, thick, obtuse; anterior part of the body stout; body not elongate. The occipital shields are always divided into two or more pieces, or entirely broken up into small shields. Two pairs of chin-shields, separated in the middle by angular scales. Only one post-ocular. Thirty to thirty-four series of scales round the neck; 209–252 scales in a lateral series between the angle of the mouth and the vent. Ventral shields nearly twice as broad as the scales of the adjoining series, 156–160 in number. Four small præ-anal shields. Fifty to fifty-three black bands across the back; they are broadest in the middle, nearly touching each other, and tapering on the sides; the yellowish ground-colour between them does not occupy more space than the bands. Generally the bands do not extend downwards to the belly, but sometimes they are continued as faint traces to the ventral shields, which are white, or, in the specimens with larger cross-bands, blackish. A more or less distinct yellowish streak on the temple. Tail black, with only two yellow transverse spots at its root."

Plate 19

HYDROPHIS NIGRA (ANDERSON).
FROM NATURE, POOREE ORISSA (REDUCED).

Length including Tail 1' 6½".
Tail 2"
Girth of Body 1¼

HYDROPHIS NIGROCINCTA
FROM NATURE IND: MUS (REDUCED)

Length including tail 1'11 Tail 2¾
Girth of Body 2¼". Girth of Neck 1½

Drawn by Annoda Prosad Bagchee, Student.

Govt Sch. of Art, Calcutta.

HYDROPHIS NIGRA (N.S.), ANDERSON.

"Neck but moderately slender, less than two-thirds the length of the body. Head broader than neck, long, with nearly straight sides, the præ-orbital equalling the temporal breadth. Snout moderately long, broad, rounded, and rather spatulate. Rostral much broader than high, its posterior extremity being on a line with the rostro-labial suture; feebly notched on its inferior margin. Nasals broader posteriorly than they are long. The third labial not in contact with the nasal, and it is almost excluded from the orbit by the fourth labial and præ-ocular. One post-ocular. The fifth and sixth labials transversely divided. Two temporals, of which the anterior is the larger. Two pairs of chin-shields, the anterior in contact, the shields of the posterior pair separated by an azygos scale. Thirty-two rows of scales round the body, slightly imbricate and smooth. Ventrals, forty-eight; the first twenty-five or so six times as large as the adjoining scales, which are rather small; the remainder diminish in size, but nearly all are distinct and undivided. Three pairs of anal-shields, of which the outer are the largest.

"Uniform intense black, without any trace of markings. Length, 19″, of which the tail is 2″. Length of snout to occiput, 0″ 7‴. Breadth across the angle of the mouth, 0″ 4‴. Breadth before the eyes, 0″ 4‴. Breadth on a line with nasal suture, 0″ 3‴. Snout to eye, 0″ 3‴. Eye to angle of mouth, two and a half lines. Angle of jaw to tip of snout, 0″ 8‴. Locality—Pooree, Cuttack."

Hydrophis Nigrocincta.

"Head small; neck slender, its length being about one-fourth of the total; body moderately elongate. Rostral shield rather broader than long; only the fourth upper labial forms the lower part of the orbit;

two post-oculars; three temporal shields on the side of each occipital. Two pairs of chin-shields, the anterior of which are in contact with each other. Twenty-seven to twenty-nine series of scales round the neck. Scales imbricate, rhombic, keeled; those on the highest side of the body as broad as long. Ventrals distinct, not quite twice as broad as the scales of the adjoining series; smooth; 320–331 in number. Four large anal-shields. The tail terminates in a large scale. The trunk is encircled by 43(53–)–61 complete rings of black colour. The width of these rings is equal on the sides and on the belly; on the vertebral line only they are a little broader; they are narrower than the interspaces, which occupy from four to five transverse series of scales, whilst a black ring occupies only three. The interspaces are greenish-olive on the back, yellowish on the sides and on the belly. The crown of the head and the upper lip are blackish, a yellow band running along the whole upper margin of the head; lower jaw whitish. Tail with from nine to eleven black cross-bars."

HYDROPHIS CORONATA.

"Head very small, twice as long as broad; neck very slender, its length being more than one-third of total. Rostral shield small, broader than long; one post-ocular; the third upper labial is not in contact with the nasal. Two pairs of chin-shields, which are in contact with each other. Nineteen to twenty-three series of scales round the neck. Scales imbricate, those on the highest part of the body higher than long, those on the sides with a small tubercle, those on the back with a keel. Ventral shields very distinct, nearly twice as large as the scales of the adjoining series, 321–337 in number, each with two small tubercles. Four anal shields, the outer of which are rather larger than the others. Trunk with from fifty-three to fifty-nine complete blackish rings, which are broader than the interspaces of the yellowish-olive ground-colour. Head and ventral side of the thin neck-like portion of the body black; the former with a yellow horseshoe-shaped mark across the frontals and nasals, and extending backwards over the superciliary edge to the temple. Tail with ten or eleven blackish cross-bars."

HYDROPHIS CHLORIS.

"Head very small, of moderate width; neck very slender, the length of the thin part of the body being more than one-third of the total. Rostral shield very small, much broader than long; one post-ocular; the third upper labial is not in contact with the nasal. Two pairs of chin-shields, in contact with each other. Thirty-one to thirty-three series of scales round the neck; scales on the back with a faint keel, and with a small tubercle near the apex. Ventral shields distinct, especially on the thin portion of the body, but not much larger than the scales of the adjoining series, 473–500 in number. Four anal shields, the outer of which are very large. Trunk greenish-olive above, yellowish on the side and below, from fifty-nine to sixty-seven rhombic blackish bands across the back, which are much narrower and fainter on the sides, and extend round the belly; their angles on the vertebral line are sometimes confluent, especially on the anterior part of the body, where the yellowish ground-colour between the cross-bands is sometimes reduced to round spots disposed in pairs. Head and anterior part of the belly entirely black. Young specimens have the markings of a deep black."

HYDROPHIS STRICTICOLLIS.

"Head narrow, not quite twice as long as broad; body slender, especially in its anterior portion. Two pairs of chin-shields, both of which are in contact with each other. Only one anterior temporal, which is as high as long. One post-ocular. Thirty-four series of scales round the neck. Ventral shields distinct, but only the anterior are twice as broad as the scales of the adjoining series; they are 398 in number. Six small præ-anal shields. Scales smooth in young specimens. Body with fifty-five blackish rings, not quite as broad as the yellowish ground-colour between them; they are rather broader and darker on the back than on the belly, and sometimes sub-interrupted in the vertebral and ventral line. Head yellow above, with irregular blackish confluent spots; whitish below. Tail with eleven blackish vertebral bars."

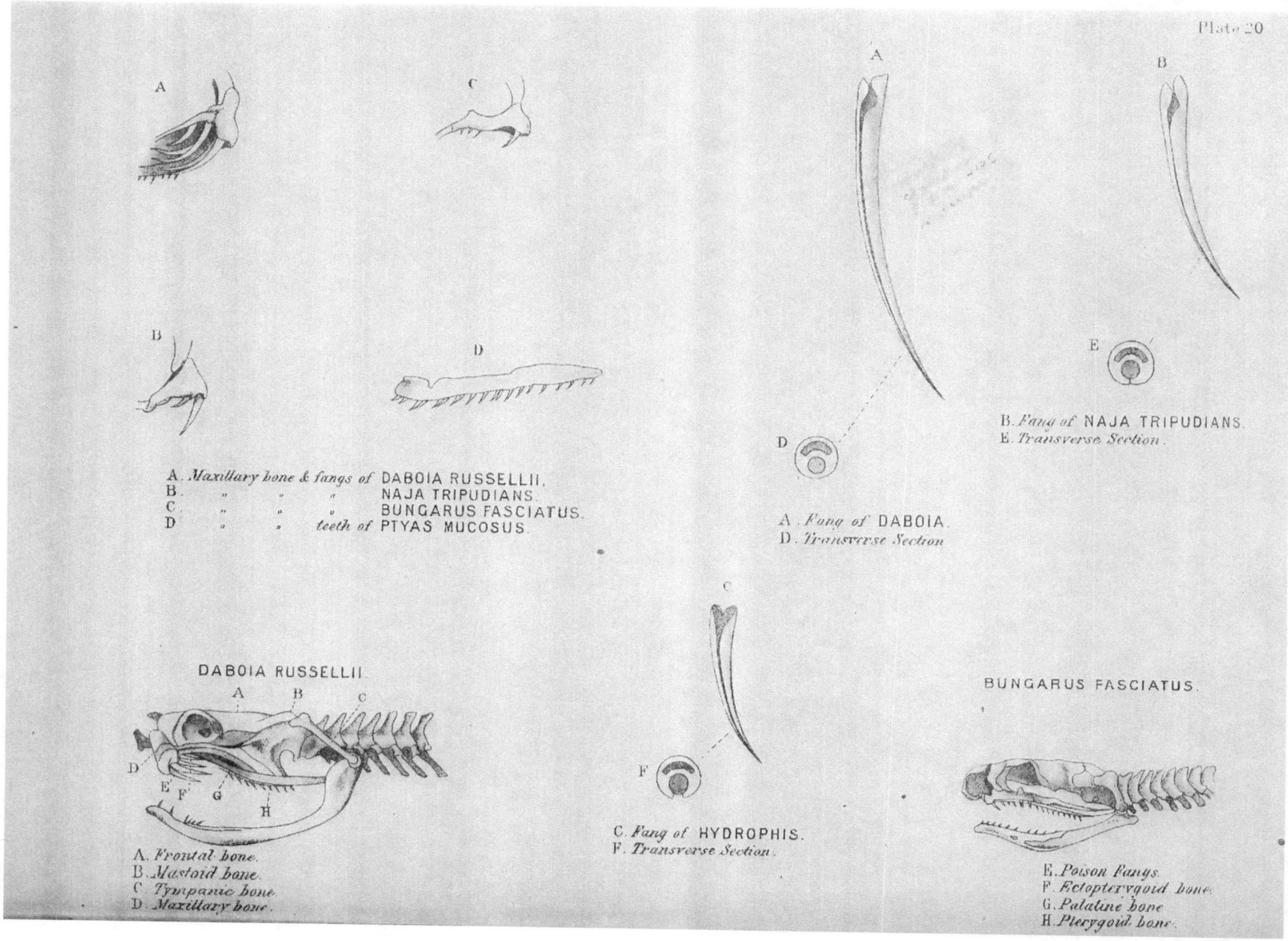
Plate 20
A
C
A
B
B
D
E
D
A. Maxillary bone & fangs of DABOIA RUSSELLII.
B. " " " NAJA TRIPUDIANS.
C. " " " BUNGARUS FASCIATUS.
D " " teeth of PTYAS MUCOSUS.
B. Fang of NAJA TRIPUDIANS.
E. Transverse Section.
A. Fang of DABOIA.
D. Transverse Section
C
DABOIA RUSSELLII.
A
B
C
D
E
F
G
H
F
BUNGARUS FASCIATUS.
A. Frontal bone.
B. Mastoid bone.
C. Tympanic bone.
D. Maxillary bone.
C. Fang of HYDROPHIS.
F. Transverse Section.
E. Poison Fangs.
F. Ectopterygoid bone.
G. Palatine bone
H. Pterygoid bone.

ARRANGEMENT OF TEETH AND FANGS.

The arrangement of the teeth and the presence or absence of fangs are of cardinal importance. Every poisonous Snake is provided with fangs, while, with one exception—and there may be others—that of *Psammodynastes pulverulentus,* innocent Snakes are free from such weapons. The manner in which the efficient and supplementary fangs are attached to the jawbone is well shown in A, B, C, whilst D demonstrates the mode in which the recurved teeth of an innocent Snake are fixed. The relations of the poison fangs and ordinary teeth are still further illustrated in the skeleton heads of the Russell's Viper (*Daboia Russellii*), *Bungarus fasciatus,* figured in Plate 20, and of the Cobra (*Naja tripudians*), in Plate 21, contrasted with the dentition displaying the simple fish-like teeth of the non-poisonous Dhamin (*Ptyas mucosus*) in Plate 21. The fangs are separately figured in A, B, C. These are either channelled into a tubular canal, as in the Daboia and Cobra, or only grooved as in the Hydrophis. It is through this tubular or grooved fang that the poison is injected from the poison-gland into the tissues of an effectively bitten animal or man.

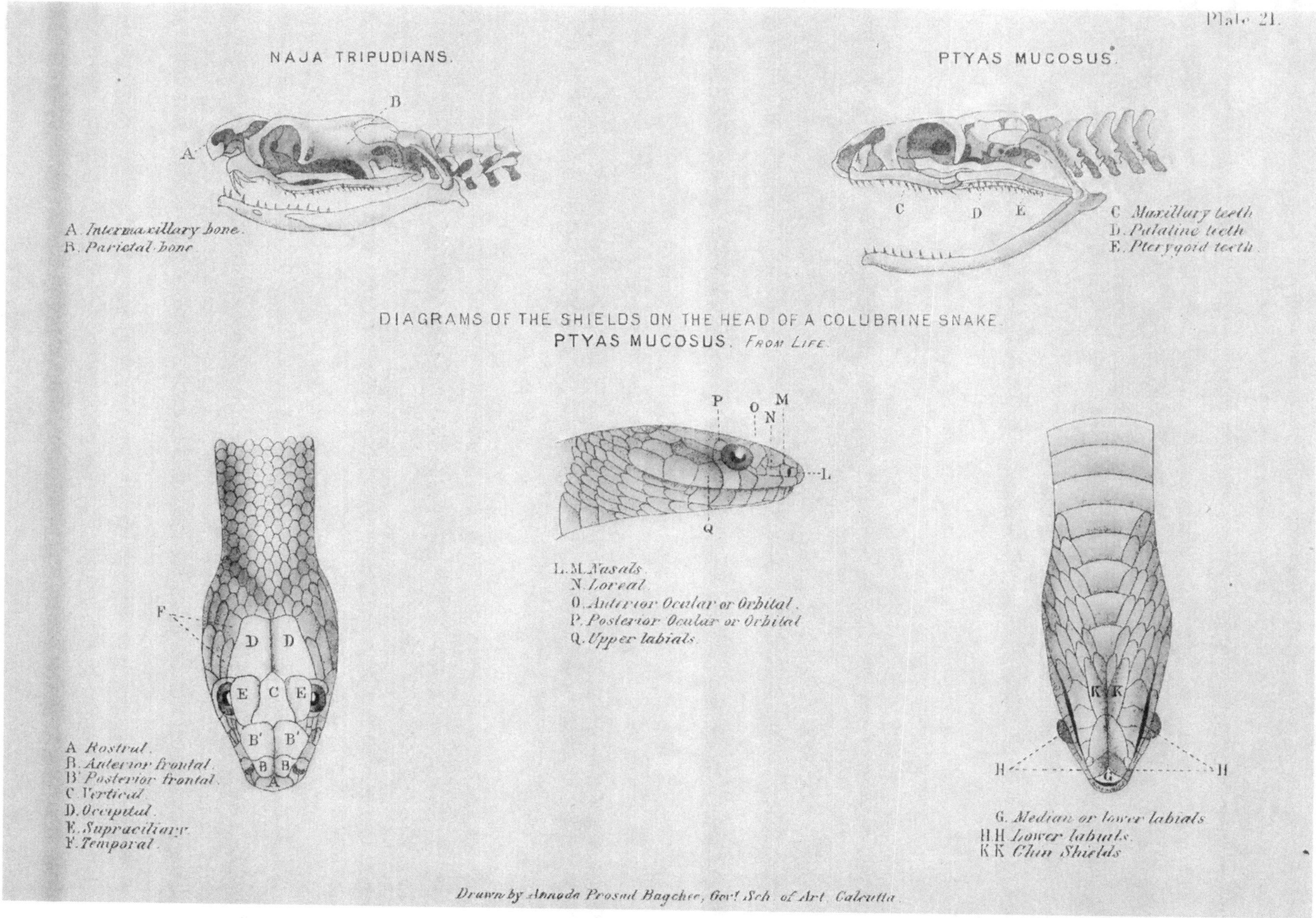
NAJA TRIPUDIANS.
A. Intermaxillary bone.
B. Parietal bone
PTYAS MUCOSUS.
C. Maxillary teeth
D. Palatine teeth
E. Pterygoid teeth.
DIAGRAMS OF THE SHIELDS ON THE HEAD OF A COLUBRINE SNAKE.
PTYAS MUCOSUS. From Life.
A. Rostral.
B. Anterior frontal.
B'. Posterior frontal.
C. Vertical.
D. Occipital.
E. Supraciliary.
F. Temporal.
L.M. Nasals.
N. Loreal.
O. Anterior Ocular or Orbital.
P. Posterior Ocular or Orbital
Q. Upper labials.
G. Median or lower labials
H.H. Lower labials.
K.K. Chin Shields
Drawn by Annoda Prosad Bagchee, Gov! Sch. of Art. Calcutta.

SHIELDS ON THE HEAD OF PTYAS MUCOSA.

The arrangement of the shields on the head of a Snake is useful for the purpose of classification and recognition. Typical examples of the various kinds of shields are illustrated in the accompanying diagrams. An explanation of the technical terms used will be found in the Glossary at the end of the work.

GLOSSARY.

Anal. Pertaining to, or situated near, the anus, or outlet.
Anterior or præ-frontal. Belonging to the forehead, or forepart.
Anterior or præ-ocular. Front portion of the region of the eye.
Azygos. Single.
Bifid. Two-cleft.
Carinated. Keel-formed.
Chin-shields. Chin coverings or protectors.
Concave. Hollow and curved, or rounded.
Coloration. The condition of colouring.
Confluent. Running one into another.
Contiguous. Touching. In actual or close contact.
Declivous. Gradually descending, sloping.
Diurnal. Relating to the day-time.
Dorsal. Pertaining to the back.
Elongate. Lengthened or stretched out.
Fœtus. Perfectly formed young in womb or egg.
Foramen. A small opening.
Genus. An assemblage of species possessing certain characters in common, by which they are distinguished from all others.
Hexagonal. Having six sides and six angles.
Hood. The dilatable portion of the neck of a poisonous Snake.
Imbricate. Lying over each other, like the tiles or shingles on a roof.
Iridescence. Exhibition of colours like those of the rainbow.
Linguate. Tongue-shaped.
Lobuliform. Having small lobed divisions.
Loreal. Space between the bill or beak and the eye.
Lower labials. Belonging to the lower lip.
Maxillary. Relating to the jaw.

Mental. Relating to the chin.

Muzzle. The projecting mouth and nose of an animal.

Nasal. Pertaining to the nose.

Nocturnal. Pertaining to, done, or occurring at night.

Obovate. Oval, with one end broader than the other.

Occipital. Pertaining to the back part of the head.

Ocellus. Spot having a resemblance to an eye.

Orbit. The cavity in which the eye is situated.

Orbital. Belonging to the cavity of the eye.

Ovate. Egg-shaped.

Oviparous. Developing young in eggs which are afterwards separated from the parent, and which are usually hatched after exclusion from the body.

Posterior or post-frontal. Belonging to back part of the forehead.

Posterior or post-ocular. Back part of the region of the eye.

Prehensile. Adapted to seize or grasp.

Recurved. Bent, or curved backward or downward.

Rostral. Pertaining to the beak.

Sinuous. Winding, crooked, undulating.

Spatulate. Shaped like a spatula or battledore.

Sub-caudal. Situated beneath the tail.

Supra-ciliary. Situated above the eyebrow.

Temporals. Pertaining to the temples of the head.

Terrestrial. Pertaining to the earth.

Trigonal. Having three angles or corners.

Truncated. Cut off; cut short; maimed.

Tubercular. Having small knobs or tubercles.

Upper labials. Belonging to the upper lip.

Variegated. Marked with different colours.

Vent. A small opening; the anus.

Ventral. Belonging to the belly.

Vertebral. Pertaining to joints of the spine, or backbone.

Vertical. Situated at the highest point, or just over the head.

Zigzag. Having short and sharp turns.